W9-ANI-574

BURUNDI

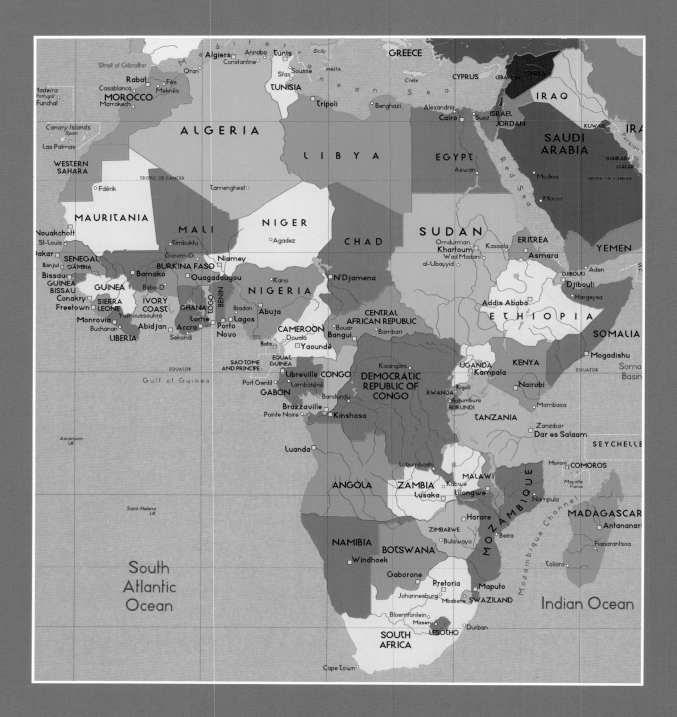

BURUNDI

Kristine Brennan

Mason Crest Publishers
Philadelphia

Produced by OTTN Publishing, Stockton, N.J.

Mason Crest Publishers
370 Reed Road
Broomall, PA 19008
www.masoncrest.com

3 5 7 9 8 6 4

Library of Congress Cataloging-in-Publication Data

  Brennan, Kristine, 1969-
    Burundi / Kristine Brennan.
       p. cm. — (Africa)
    Includes bibliographical references and index.
    ISBN 1-59084-820-9
    1. Burundi—Juvenile literature. I. Title. II. Series.

    DT450.54.B74 2004
    967.572—dc22

                                        2004007111

Table of Contents

Africa: Continent in the Balance
Robert I. Rotberg

Africa is the cradle of humankind, but for millennia it was off the familiar, beaten path of global commerce and discovery. Its many peoples therefore developed largely apart from the diffusion of modern knowledge and the spread of technological innovation until the 17th through 19th centuries. With the coming to Africa of the book, the wheel, the hoe, and the modern rifle and cannon, foreigners also brought the vastly destructive transatlantic slave trade, oppression, discrimination, and onerous colonial rule. Emerging from that crucible of European rule, Africans created nationalistic movements and then claimed their numerous national independences in the 1960s. The result is the world's largest continental assembly of new countries.

There are 53 members of the African Union, a regional political grouping, and 48 of those nations lie south of the Sahara. Fifteen of them, including mighty Ethiopia, are landlocked, making international trade and economic growth that much more arduous and expensive. Access to navigable rivers is limited, natural harbors are few, soils are poor and thin, several countries largely consist of miles and miles of sand, and tropical diseases have sapped the strength and productivity of innumerable millions. Being landlocked, having few resources (although countries along Africa's west coast have tapped into deep offshore petroleum and gas reservoirs), and being beset by malaria, tuberculosis, schistosomiasis, AIDS, and many other maladies has kept much of Africa poor for centuries.

Thirty-two of the world's poorest 44 countries are African. Hunger is common. So is rapid deforestation and desertification. Unemployment rates are often over 50 percent, for jobs are few—even in agriculture. Where Africa once

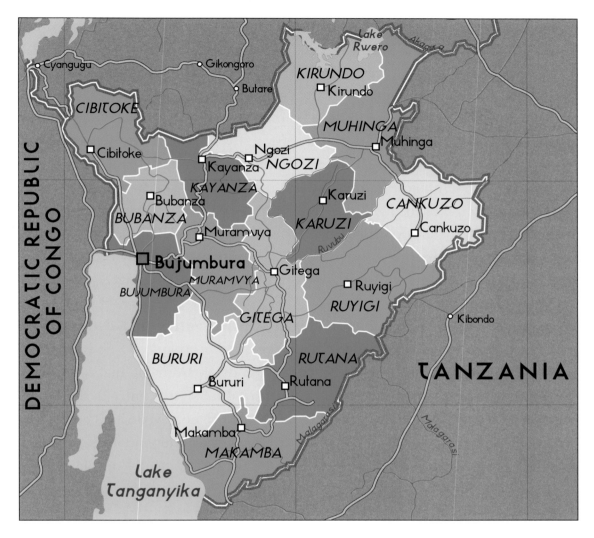

Burundi, in Central Africa, is divided into 16 provinces.

was a land of small villages and a few large cities, with almost everyone engaged in growing grain or root crops or grazing cattle, camels, sheep, and goats, today more than half of all the more than 750 million Africans, especially those who live south of the Sahara, reside in towns and cities. Traditional agriculture hardly pays, and a number of countries in Africa—particularly the smaller and more fragile ones—can no longer feed themselves.

There is not one Africa, for the continent is full of contradictions and variety. Of the 675 million people living south of the Sahara, at least 130 million live in Nigeria, 67 million in Ethiopia, 55 million in the Democratic Republic of the Congo, and 45 million in South Africa. By contrast, tiny Djibouti and Equatorial Guinea have fewer than 1 million people each, and prosperous Botswana and Namibia each are under 2 million in population. Within some countries, even medium-sized ones like Zambia (11 million), there are a plethora of distinct ethnic groups speaking separate languages. Zambia, typical with its multitude of competing entities, has 70 such peoples, roughly broken down into four language and cultural zones. Three of those languages jostle with English for primacy.

Given the kaleidoscopic quality of African culture and deep-grained poverty, it is no wonder that Africa has developed economically and politically less rapidly than other regions. Since independence from colonial rule, weak governance has also plagued Africa and contributed significantly to the widespread poverty of its peoples. Only Botswana and offshore Mauritius have been governed democratically without interruption since independence. Both are among Africa's wealthiest countries, too, thanks to the steady application of good governance.

Aside from those two nations, and South Africa, Africa has been a continent of coups since 1960, with massive and oil-rich Nigeria suffering incessant periods of harsh, corrupt, autocratic military rule. Nearly every other country on or around the continent, small and large, has been plagued by similar bouts of instability and dictatorial rule. In the 1970s and 1980s Idi Amin ruled Uganda capriciously and Jean-Bedel Bokassa proclaimed himself emperor of the Central African Republic. Macias Nguema of Equatorial Guinea was another in that same mold. More recently Daniel arap Moi held Kenya in thrall and Robert Mugabe has imposed himself on once-prosperous Zimbabwe. In both of those cases, as in the case of Gnassingbe Eyadema in Togo and the late Mobutu Sese Seko in Congo, these presidents stole wildly and drove entire peoples and their nations into penury. Corruption is common in Africa, and so are a weak rule-of-law framework, misplaced development, high expenditures on soldiers and low expenditures on health and education, and a widespread (but not universal) refusal on the part of leaders to work well for their followers and citizens.

Conflict between groups within countries has also been common in Africa. More than 12 million Africans have been killed in the civil wars of Africa since 1990, with more than 3 million losing their lives in Congo and more than 2 million in the Sudan. War between north and south has been constant in the Sudan since 1981. In 2003 there were serious ongoing hostilities in northeastern Congo, Burundi, Angola, Liberia, Guinea, Ivory Coast, the Central African Republic, and Guinea-Bissau, and a coup (later reversed) in São Tomé and Príncipe.

Despite such dangers, despotism, and decay, Africa is improving. Botswana and Mauritius, now joined by South Africa, Senegal, Kenya, and Ghana, are beacons of democratic growth and enlightened rule. Uganda and Senegal are taking the lead in combating and reducing the spread of AIDS, and others are following. There are serious signs of the kinds of progressive economic policy changes that might lead to prosperity for more of Africa's peoples. The trajectory in Africa is positive.

Most of Burundi is rolling grassland that is ideal for farming and raising cattle. (Opposite) A herdsman looks out at the rolling hills. (Right) These Burundian fishermen are standing on the shores of Lake Tanganyika, one of the longest and deepest freshwater lakes in the world.

1 The Land of a Thousand Hills

BWAKEYE! ARE YOU ready to discover Burundi? This is how the people of this tiny country in east central Africa greet each other in the official language, Kirundi. Until the 1990s, relatively few Americans had heard of Burundi. Unfortunately, the reason many people know about the country today is that it has suffered more than a decade of brutal fighting between two ethnic groups. These are the Hutu, who make up about 85 percent of the population, and the Tutsi, who are about 14 percent of the population. During the civil war in Burundi hundreds of thousands of people have been killed, and more than a million were displaced or fled the country as refugees.

Although the Republic of Burundi has a bloody history, the country itself has great natural beauty, featuring rich red volcanic soil and lush green hills. Burundi is part of Africa's Great Lakes Region, so named for the six large lakes that dot the area (Lake Albert, Lake George, Lake Edward, Lake Victoria, Lake Kivu, and Lake Tanganyika). Although Burundi controls the northern shore of Lake Tanganyika, which is the world's longest freshwater lake, the country is *landlocked*. Its total area is 10,745 square miles (27,830 square kilometers), making it slightly smaller than the state of Maryland.

The capital of Burundi is Bujumbura, which is in the province of the same name. This city is home to Burundi's only functioning port, located on Lake Tanganyika's northern shore. The Ruzizi River and Lake Tanganyika make up Burundi's western border with the Democratic Republic of the Congo (DRC). Tanzania is Burundi's neighbor to the east.

It is Burundi's neighbor to the north, however, with which it has the most in common. Rwanda is another small country with approximately the same ethnic makeup as Burundi, and many of the same cultural traditions. In both countries, the Hutu majority and the Tutsi minority have been killing each other for decades. In Rwanda the Hutu once dominated the government, but in Burundi the Tutsi minority have long controlled the political scene.

A Varied Landscape

Despite its small size, Burundi is a land of varied natural attributes. To the west, there is the Ruzizi plain, a narrow strip along Ruzizi River. The plain and the shores of Lake Tanganyika have the lowest elevation in Burundi, at about 2,533 feet (772 meters). Mount Heha is the country's highest point, at 8,760 feet (2,670 m). The terrain of central Burundi is *savanna*, a grassland with low rolling hills that is ideal for grazing cattle. Other parts of Burundi's interior are swampy and dotted with salt marshes.

Quick Facts: The Geography of Burundi

Location: Central Africa, east of Democratic Republic of Congo.

Area: (slightly smaller than Maryland)
total: 10,745 square miles (27,830 sq. km)
land: 9,903 square miles (25,650 sq. km)
water: 2,873 square miles (7,444 sq. km)

Borders: Democratic Republic of the Congo, 145 miles (233 km); Rwanda, 180 miles (290 km); Tanzania, 280 miles (451 km).

Climate: equatorial; high plateau with generally moderate temperatures.

Terrain: hilly and mountainous, dropping to a plateau in east, some plains.

Elevation extremes:
lowest point: Lake Tanganyika, 2,533 feet (772 m)
highest point: Mount Heha, 8,760 feet (2,670 m)

Natural hazards: flooding, landslides, drought.

Source: CIA World Factbook, 2003.

Temperatures in Burundi do not vary much. Daytime temperatures generally range from about 62° to 74° Fahrenheit (17° to 23° Celsius). The mountainous areas are the coolest; the warmest and most humid part of Burundi is located in the southwestern area around Lake Tanganyika.

The comfortable, mild climate may be one reason for the tiny country's high population density. This hilly land is home to more than 6 million people, with an average of more than 600 people per square mile (nearly 250 people per square kilometer), the second-highest population density in Africa after Rwanda. (By comparison, the average population density of the United States is about 76 people per square mile, or 27 people per square kilometer.) Most of the people live in small rural farming communities. There are only two major cities in Burundi, Bujumbura and Gitega.

One reason Burundi's climate is ideal for agriculture is its two rainy seasons. These last from February to May and from September to November. Dry seasons are shorter, running from June to August and December to January. Each year the country gets an average of approximately 59 inches (150 centimeters) of rainfall. Burundi's main natural hazards are flooding, drought, landslides, and hailstorms.

Burundi was once heavily forested, but now the little forest that remains in Burundi is being cut down for wood to use as fuel or building material. Trees are not being replanted in great enough numbers to stem deforestation.

Wildlife

Burundi is part of the Albertine Rift, a zone of great *biodiversity* extending from the northern end of Lake Albert to the southern end of Lake Tanganyika and extending through the countries of Uganda, Rwanda, Democratic Republic of the Congo, Burundi, and Tanzania. The Albertine Rift is home to numerous *endemic* or nearly endemic species of plants, birds, and mammals. Fish are plentiful in Lake Tanganyika; the hippopotamus, on the other hand, is now a very rare resident of the lake and Burundi's rivers. Crocodiles flourish in lakes and rivers, although a rare sharp-nosed variety of crocodile has probably disappeared from the republic's waters.

Most wildlife in Burundi has become a casualty of human population growth. The years of ethnic fighting have also created conditions that make survival difficult for both people and animals. Mammals and birds have not fared well in Burundi. Once there were herds of elephants, but they have long since been hunted to near-extinction, and the few that remain are limit-

Hippopotamuses can still be found in a nature reserve in the western part of Burundi, but they have mostly vanished from other parts of the country.

ed to game preserves. There were once chimpanzees living near the shores of Lake Tanganyika and the mountainous areas near Rwanda, but their homes have been destroyed by the unrest in both countries.

In addition to competing with human settlement, the birds and animals also risk being hunted to extinction as food. Because more than three-fifths of Burundi's population is impoverished, and hundreds of thousands of people have been internally displaced during Burundi's chaotic modern history, people eat whatever they can catch. Such game birds as partridges, quail, guinea hens, ducks, and geese still survive in the area around the lake, but these species have been heavily hunted.

To see what Burundi's forests and wildlife once looked like, the best place to go is a nature preserve near the border with the Democratic Republic of the Congo. There, visitors can see crocodiles, hippos, antelope, wild boars, monkeys, and lemurs as well as various birds. Unfortunately, the country has few resources to dedicate to manage its once-rich and varied flora and fauna.

(Opposite) A Tutsi boy with one of the longhorn cattle that are so important in Tutsi society. The Tutsi arrived in Burundi during the 14th and 15th centuries. (Right) A relative of slain Burundian president Melchior Ndadaye holds his photograph at his October 1993 funeral. The assassination of Ndadaye touched off a decade-long civil war that devastated Burundi.

2 From Kingdom to Republic

LITTLE IS KNOWN ABOUT the earliest inhabitants of the region today known as Burundi. Most scholars believe the Hutu (or Wahutu) people inhabited the Great Lakes region of central Africa by 1000 A.D. The Hutu established permanent homes and fed themselves mainly through farming. Some of their crops included grains like sorghum and *eleusine*, corn, beans and yams, and a root vegetable called taro. Around the 14th or 15th centuries, the Hutu started cultivating banana trees, and they soon became expert banana-growers.

The Hutu were not the only inhabitants of Burundi. A people of pygmy ancestry called the Twa (or Batwa) lived in smaller groups than did the Hutu. Unlike the Hutu, they were nomadic hunter-gatherers who lived in forested areas. The Twa were always a small group; today, they are believed to make up about 1 percent of Burundi's population.

During the 14th and 15th centuries, a new group of Africans migrated into Burundi, the Tutsi. The Tutsi herded longhorn humpbacked sanga cattle, and relied on the herds to provide milk, hides, and meat. For the Tutsi, cattle were a mobile and readily exchangeable form of wealth. They did not have to settle in one place and wait for their crops to grow in order to trade for the things they wanted. Also, during times of drought it was far easier for Tutsi herders to move their cattle in search of fresh grassland than it was for the Hutu farmers to move and establish new family farms.

All of these people spoke a Bantu language called Kirundi (or Rundi), and for the most part they lived together harmoniously. The people of Burundi lived by a clan system, which permitted members of different ethnic groups to live together in the same clan. People could be bound together by family, social affairs, friendship, or religion. Some clans were considered more prestigious than others because they controlled a piece of sacred land, for example.

Gradually, the Hutu and Tutsi developed a *client-patron relationship*. This social contract developed because when the Hutus' crops failed, they still needed to eat and wanted to live in the safety of a community. Sometimes, the price of food and safety was becoming a caretaker for a Tutsi herdsman's cattle. The word *hutu* means "peasant" in Kirundi, but even someone of Tutsi birth could become a Hutu by entering into an agreement to serve someone in exchange for food, land, or shelter.

Precolonial Society in Burundi

Burundi had some two million inhabitants by the 18th century. They were distributed in communities isolated from one another by steep hills, but controlled by one *mwami* (king), who was a Tutsi. The first *mwami* to ascend the throne in Burundi was Ntare Rushatsi I, who came to power around 1650. Ntare Rushatsi believed that he was born containing a seed that set him apart from ordinary people and gave him authority to rule.

The royal courts were set up like small cities. The residence of the *mwami* was the largest and tallest house, and it was surrounded by other homes. The more important or influential a person was in the kingdom, the larger his family's house. The king would receive visitors, settle disputes, and meet with his advisors in his home.

A system of local chiefs and judges supported the *mwami*'s rule, because populations in the kingdom were widely dispersed. The chiefs handled matters of defense, while the judges settled local disputes. Although most of the chiefs were Tutsi, there were also some Hutu chiefs and "hill judges" who were esteemed as the wise men of their communities. Chiefs would go out into the surrounding countryside and collect tribute for the king. These could take the form of baskets of sorghum, honey, or more specialized offerings from honored families. These offerings, called **inkuka**, often made use of a person's special talents, or were repayment to the *mwami* for a special favor. For example, *inkuka* might be ironwork from a blacksmith, or a calf born from a cow given to a family by the king.

The *mwami*'s descendants were a class of Tutsi princes of royal blood called the Ganwa. The Ganwa princes were assigned to oversee a satellite kingdom in remote area that the *mwami* wished to secure or conquer. Sometimes, they challenged the *mwami*'s power and tried to seize a larger piece of the kingdom. In those cases, the king relied on his chiefs to keep the upstart princes in check.

With the rise of the Tutsi kings, the distinctions between Hutu and Tutsi became more pronounced. Only Tutsi could milk the king's cows, for instance, while Hutu kept track of royal grain stores.

European Contact

The English explorer John Hanning Speke was one of the first Europeans to explore the Burundi area, visiting Lake Tanganyika in 1858. Within 45 years Germany would control the region as a colony called Ruanda-Urundi.

Although there was already an imbalance of power between the Tutsi and the Hutu, the arrival of Europeans during the 19th century deepened the disparity. European countries wanted to control African lands because the natural resources of Africa would help them add to their vast empires. Although parts of North, South, and West Africa came under European control in the 16th and 17th centuries, Europeans did not arrive in Central Africa until much later. The first Europeans to set foot in present-day Burundi may have been the English explorers Richard Burton and John Hanning Speke. In 1858, while on a mission for the Royal Geographical Society to find the source of the Nile River, they briefly stopped on Lake Tanganyika's north shore. The Scottish explorer Joseph Thomson followed them to the region. In 1871, two Roman Catholic priests from Germany started a mission in Bujumbura. Protestant missionaries from England reached the region after them.

In order to avoid a conflict among the European nations over Africa, Great Britain, France, Belgium, Germany, and other major colonial powers met in Berlin during 1884–85 to decide how to divide the continent among themselves. Each of the major powers was granted a *sphere of influence* over a part of Africa. Germany was given control over Burundi, as well as neighboring Rwanda. In 1894, the first representative of the German government, Count Gustav Adolf von Gotzen, arrived in Burundi to claim it as a German colony.

When the Germans arrived, the kingdom was in the midst of a civil war. Mwami Mwezi Gisabo had ruled Burundi for decades, but his sons, brothers, and nephews were fighting him for power. The Germans promised to support Mwezi Gisabo as king of Burundi if he would agree to German authority over the kingdom. To maintain his power, in 1903 Mwezi Gisabo reluctantly signed the Treaty of Kiganda, which made Burundi a German colony.

The system of *indirect rule* marked the end of real power for Burundi's kings. After Gisabo died in 1908, his young son assumed the throne, but he was a figurehead with little authority. The real power lay with the German governor of the region, who oversaw the management of Rwanda and Burundi, which was then known as Ruanda-Urundi.

During World War I (1914–18), Germany's colonies in Africa came under attack. In 1916 Belgian troops from neighboring Congo invaded Ruanda-Urundi, overwhelmed the German forces, and effectively took control over Burundi. After the war ended, the League of Nations, a newly formed international association of states, gave Belgium a mandate to control Burundi.

During the time Burundi was under Belgian rule, cultivation of such crops as coffee, tea, and *cassava* became profitable industries. Exports of these products allowed the tiny country to begin participating in international trade. However, the Burundian farmers who did the actual work of raising the crops were underpaid or even unpaid. The Belgian administrators told the farmers what crops they had to plant on their personal plots of land.

Although there had always been a level of antagonism between Hutu and Tutsi, it grew worse during the 40 years of Belgian rule. The Europeans treated the Tutsi better than they did the Hutu or Twa, characterizing the Tutsi as tall and aristocratic. For example, Pierre Ryckmans, the Belgian administrator in Burundi from 1920 to 1925, described the Tutsi as "destined to rule." Hutu, on the other hand, were described as being short and squat, with lower intellects and less dignity. These generalizations failed to take into account that intermarriage made it impossible to tell who belonged to which ethnic group. Ethnicity is *patrilineal* in Burundi: the child of a Tutsi father and a Hutu mother is considered a Tutsi.

During the 1920s the Belgians insisted everyone had to carry identification cards that indicated whether they were Hutu or Tutsi. Because the Tutsi were favored, most of the children who attended schools in Burundi were Tutsi, and educated Tutsi were given most of the civil service jobs in the Belgian administration.

Independence

The end of World War II marked the decline of Belgian control over Burundi. In 1946, the United Nations told Belgium to begin preparing Burundi for independence. However, Belgium moved slowly, and by the late 1950s many people in Burundi were demanding their freedom. In 1958 Louis Rwagasore, the oldest son of the *mwami*, formed a political party with the goal of self-determination for Burundi. Rwagasore had been educated in Belgium, and his Party of National Unity and Progress (Union pour le progres national, or UPRONA) appealed to both Hutu and Tutsi with strong nationalist feelings.

Rwagasore hoped to unite the country ethnically as well as politically. Although he was a Tutsi member of the Ganwa class of ruling princes, in 1959 he married a Hutu woman. That same year his father, Mwami Mwambutsa IV, demanded that Burundi be granted immediate independence.

The Belgian administrator of Burundi tried to forbid Rwagasore from participating in politics. The Belgian government helped create a rival faction, the Christian Democratic Party (Parti democrate chretien, or PDC), which was headed by two sons of a chief who disagreed with Mwambutsa's opposition to continued Belgian rule. More than two dozen other political parties were established during the next two years.

In September 1961, the United Nations supervised Burundi's first election. UPRONA candidates won 58 of the 64 seats in a new National Assembly, and Louis Rwagasore was elected the *prime minister* by a wide margin. However, he

Burundi achieved independence under Mwami Mwambutsa IV. The last king of Burundi ruled until 1965, when his government was overthrown and the country declared a republic.

would never complete his goal of unifying the country. A month after the election, Rwagasore was assassinated by two rivals from the Christian Democratic Party.

Burundi officially became independent on July 1, 1962. Mwambutsa appointed a string of prime ministers over the next few years, starting with his own cousin, a Tutsi aristocrat named André Muhirwa. Mwambutsa tried to appeal to both ethnic groups, next naming a Hutu named Pierre Ngendandumwe prime minister. A Tutsi named Albin Nyamoya was next. In 1965, he reinstalled Ngendandumwe as Burundi's prime minister, but the Hutu politician was assassinated a few months later.

In elections held in May 1965, UPRONA candidates again won most seats in the national assembly. Two-thirds of the candidates were Hutu, and they wanted a Hutu prime minister. When Mwambutsa chose an elderly Tutsi chief named Leopold Biha, the Hutu leadership was angered. Hutu army officers attempted to overthrow the government, and Hutu massacred hundreds of Tutsi. However, the coup failed and a Tutsi military leader named Michel Micombero ordered the army to take revenge. In retaliation, the Tutsi-dominated army murdered at least 2,000 Hutu.

Mwami Mwambutsa fled the country. Although he attempted to rule from neighboring Congo, he gave up the throne under pressure from his ambitious son, Ntare V, who declared himself the head of state in Burundi. Micombero had helped Ntare V gain power, but in 1966, while the new *mwami* was out of the country on a diplomatic visit, he staged a coup of his own. Micombero abolished the monarchy, declared Burundi a republic, and named himself president.

Unrest in Burundi

Micombero set about consolidating his control over Burundi. He made UPRONA the only legal political party and removed Hutu from government and military positions. In 1971, he put Hutu and some Tutsi accused of remaining loyal to the king on trial in Muramvya. On his orders, the army kept Hutu from participating in government, schools, or military service through systematic intimidation and harassment.

On April 29, 1972, Hutu rebels tried to overthrow Micombero's government. Thousands of Tutsi in Bujumbura and elsewhere were killed in the revolt. Micombero and his administration survived, however, and took revenge during May and June 1972. The army swept through Burundi, slaughtering Hutu. Those with education, money, or leadership roles in their communities were particularly targeted. By the time this *ikiza* ("scourge") had come to its bloody conclusion, an estimated 150,000 people were dead, and hundreds of thousands more had fled their homes.

Micombero held the presidency until 1976, when he was deposed by one of his own henchman, Colonel Jean-Baptiste Bagaza. Although Bagaza was a Tutsi, he promised not to order any massacres against the Hutu and declared that those who had fled during the *ikiza* had nothing to fear if they returned to Burundi.

Some Hutu refugees returned, but many ignored the invitation. Instead, they began planning rebellion from exile. In Rwanda, refugees founded the Front for Democracy in Burundi (FRODEBU) during the late 1970s. A more extreme group called Party for the Liberation of the Hutu People (PALIPHE-

HUTU) developed in a Tanzanian refugee camp in 1980. Other opposition groups would follow in short order.

Although there were no massacres while Bagaza ruled Burundi, the Hutu remained second-class citizens. Most Hutu were afraid to send their children to school, so for a generation the Tutsi were the only group with access to education. Spying on ordinary citizens was common during the Bagaza presidency, and freedom of the press was nonexistent. Bagaza found fault with the Catholic church in particular, accusing the clergy of stirring up international sympathy for the Hutu and casting his government in a negative light. From 1985 to 1987, he tried to drive Catholic clergy and missionaries out of Burundi by enacting laws that forbade prayer groups and by arresting and detaining some clergy without trial. However, when Bagaza tried to eliminate military officers who were not loyal to him, he lost the support of the army. He was overthrown in a military coup, and fled to Libya in 1987.

Burundi's new president was another Tutsi, Major Pierre Buyoya. He dismissed the National Assembly and established his own panel of 31 representatives, called the Military Committee for National Salvation, to govern Burundi. Buyoya did take some small but encouraging steps to unite the country. He ended the persecution of Catholic priests and missionaries, and he appointed civilians—even a few Hutu—to the council of ministers. However, he did nothing to allay a widespread fear among Tutsi that the Hutu were waiting to avenge the 1972 mass killings.

In August of 1988, extremists from PALIPHEHUTU confirmed the Tutsi fears. They led Hutu farmers in an armed attack on Tutsi in the northern provinces of Ngozi and Kirundo. The rebels justified their attack as pre-

Throughout Burundi's history there have been incidents of violence between Hutu and Tutsi. This photograph shows the half-buried body of a Hutu man massacred in the first weeks of the 1993 civil war.

venting a Tutsi plan to exterminate the Hutu. Buyoya's army crushed this rebellion swiftly, but some observers estimated that casualties were as high as 20,000. The world community denounced his harsh treatment of the Hutu rebels, and the United States and other countries imposed *sanctions* on Burundi in response to this violence.

To regain the support of the world community for his regime, Buyoya enacted a series of reforms between 1991 and 1993. He had a new democratic constitution written, appointed a Hutu named Adrien Sibomana as prime minister, and restored the National Assembly, in which Tutsi and Hutu were given equal representation. Buyoya permitted political parties, such as FRODEBU, to campaign in the country. He also signed into law a document called the Charter of Unity, which condemned ethnic discrimination and fighting, and called for direct presidential and legislative elections to take place in June 1993.

Buyoya permitted direct elections because he believed he would win. His confidence proved to be unfounded, however. The FRODEBU candidate, a Hutu named Melchior Ndadaye, became Burundi's first democratically elected president. When FRODEBU candidates also took a majority of the National Assembly seats in elections, many of the Tutsi elite, who had traditionally controlled the government, felt that their authority was threatened. Furthermore, they feared for their lives if Ndadaye's plan to invite Hutu refugees to return to Burundi came to pass. Although Buyoya handed over power without incident, the tensions between the two groups did not dissipate.

On the night of October 20, 1993, rebellious Tutsi soldiers attacked Burundi's presidential palace. President Ndadaye was abducted and later killed, as was the vice president and other ministers. Prime Minister Sylvie Kinigi, a moderate Tutsi of the UPRONA party, tried to preserve what was left of Ndadaye's administration, and after the coup failed the military pledged its support to her.

Attacks on Tutsi civilians began immediately after the news of President Ndadaye's assassination. They were surrounded and slaughtered at schools, markets, and other public places. The Tutsi-dominated army swung into action, first to protect the Tutsi, then to avenge their slaughter. The resulting civil war lasted well into the 21st century, and approximately 200,000 people were killed—most of them innocent civilians. "From nine in the evening to five in the morning, everybody in Burundi stayed indoors," observed Christian Jennings, a reporter in Burundi at the peak of civil war in 1994. "The only people abroad were those for whom the night is killing time."

The number of casualties does not take into account the estimated 1.3 million Burundians who have fled the country. In many cases, refugees had no homes left to flee when they ran. Houses in both Hutu and Tutsi neighborhoods were destroyed when towns came under attack by the army or by rebel groups. The displaced Tutsi moved to camps that were under the protection of the army; the dispersed Hutu were more likely to hide in the bush and sneak out to cultivate their land at night if they had managed to hide near their original homes. For those who ran for Tanzania, Uganda, Rwanda, or the Democratic Republic of the Congo, crowded and unsanitary refugee camps awaited them. Some refugees—mostly Hutu—died of starvation, disease, or animal attacks as they were trying to escape from Burundi.

(Opposite) Nelson Mandela (left) shakes hands with Tutsi Pierre Buyoya during an April 2003 ceremony in which Buyoya turned the presidency of Burundi's transitional government over to a Hutu, Domitien Ndayizeye. (Right) The African Union Force, a peacekeeping army, has cracked down on Hutu rebels fighting the government.

3 A Government in Turmoil

SINCE THE ASSASSINATION of Burundi's first democratically elected president in October 1993, hundreds of thousands of Burundians were killed, internally displaced, or became refugees in neighboring countries. There have been several efforts to make peace in the country and establish a national government. However, rebel groups have often disagreed with the ruling party and the prospects for sustained peace are uncertain.

The government of Burundi has been in turmoil since the assassination of Ndadaye. Prime minister Sylvie Kinigi acted as interim president until Cyprien Ntaryamira, a Hutu from the FRODEBU party, was officially named president of Burundi on January 13, 1994. However, his new administration never took shape. On April 6, 1994, an airplane carrying Ntaryamira and Rwandan President Juvenal Habyarimana crashed over Kigali, the capital of Rwanda, killing everyone on board.

Six months earlier the United Nations had sent a Mauritanian diplomat named Ahmedou Ould-Abdallah to Burundi as an advisor to the newly elected officials—many of whom lacked experience in politics—as they struggled to establish the government's authority and end violence. When the death of Habyarimana, a Rwandan Hutu, spurred widespread violence against Tutsi in that country, Ould-Abdallah feared a similar outbreak of violence in Burundi. He appeared on Burundian national television and supported the FRODEBU leader next in line for the presidency according to the new Burundian constitution. That leader was another Hutu, Sylvestre Ntibantunganya.

The U.N. envoy's plan worked. Ntibantunganya became interim president, and the violence in Burundi did not become as widespread as in Rwanda, where between April and July 1994 approximately 800,000 Tutsi and moderate Hutu were massacred. In September 1994 12 of Burundi's 13 recognized political parties signed a document called the Convention of Government. This was a power-sharing pact between Hutu and Tutsi politicians. Control over the government would be evenly divided between Hutu and Tutsi. If the president were a Hutu, for instance, then the prime minister would be a Tutsi. Ntibantunganya was sworn in as Burundi's president on October 1, 1994. Anatole Kanyenkiko served as prime minister, but within a few months he resigned and was replaced by another Tutsi from UPRONA, Antoine Nduwayo.

The Convention of Government did not end the struggle for power, and Burundi slid back into chaos. President Ntibantunganya was not supported by the military, and he feared for his life. He survived a 1996 assassination attempt in which Burundian soldiers fired at his motorcade with an antitank rocket but hit the wrong car. Throughout 1995 and 1996, FRODEBU leaders were assassinated regularly; others went into exile.

The United Nations withdrew the discouraged envoy Ahmedou Ould-Abdallah in October 1995. In March 1996 the African statesman Julius Nyerere, who had led Tanzania to independence in the 1960s and served as that country's first president until 1985, was given a formidable task by the U.N.: to bring peace to Burundi. On June 25, he invited Burundian leaders, including president Ntibantunganya and prime minister Nduwayo, to a meeting in Arusha, Tanzania. At the conference, the United Nations offered to send military help to Burundi to secure the peace. Unfortunately, the idea of military intervention by outsiders upset both Hutu and Tutsi. The Arusha summit was a failure that helped make a bad situation worse.

A delegate to the 2003 Burundi peace talks in Dar es Salaam, Tanzania, expresses the hopes of many Africans.

The situation deteriorated completely on July 25, 1996, when military leaders declared the presidency vacant and named the former president Pierre Buyoya to fill the top leadership position. With military support

Buyoya *nullified* the Convention of Government, made political parties illegal, broke up the National Assembly, and invalidated the constitution. In August, Burundi's neighbors Rwanda and Tanzania imposed *sanctions* against the country in an effort to get Buyoya to restore Burundi's constitution and to negotiate with Hutu extremists. Buyoya restored the National Assembly in October, and allowed political parties to resume some of their activities. In return, Burundi's neighbors relaxed the sanctions in 1997.

In 1998 Buyoya was officially sworn in as president, despite the opposition of exiled FRODEBU party leader Jean Minani. Buyoya tried to win Hutu support by appointing a Hutu named Pascal-Firmin Ndimara prime minister, and he also included a few Hutu in his cabinet. The administration adopted a new constitution, which Buyoya stressed was intended to be transitional until democracy could be implemented. However, Buyoya angered Hutu by his efforts to crack down on people opposed to his government. Under his direction the military implemented a policy of taking rural Hutu families from their homes and driving them into camps where soldiers could observe their actions and make sure they were not conspiring against the government. This practice became known as *regroupment*.

In backlash against the military's disregard for the rights of Hutu, various Hutu rebel groups fought back against the government and the Tutsi. The largest insurgent group fighting against the government was the Forces for Defense of Democracy (FDD); smaller groups included PALIPHEHUTU and the Front for National Liberation (FROLINA). These insurgent groups of Hutu attacked Tutsi civilians to express their frustration with the Tutsi-dominated government.

When the international organization Human Rights Watch visited Burundi in 1997, it found that both Tutsi and Hutu civilians were afraid of random violence and displacement from their homes. People feared that if they appeared to support the insurgents, the army would kill them, but if they refused to support the rebel groups, they would be murdered for collaborating with the military.

Efforts to Broker Peace in Burundi

Hutu and Tutsi were weary of fighting as the 20th century drew to a close. In June 1998 Julius Nyerere convened a new series of peace talks in Arusha. Representatives from most of Burundi's political parties attended, but Nyerere only managed to get them to agree to negotiate in the future. Although members of the FDD and FROLINA attended the first meeting, they dropped out of the process when the other delegates refused to meet their demands.

After Nyerere died in 1999, former South African president and Nobel Peace Prize winner Nelson Mandela took over the Arusha talks. Mandela met with the FDD and FROLINA in an attempt to bring them back to the talks. One of their demands was an end to the army's *regroupment* program. Buyoya suspended the policy, but the two rebel groups never did return to Arusha, choosing to continue attacking civilians.

Mandela kept the pressure on the delegates at Arusha until the different groups reached an agreement in the summer of 2000. On August 28, 2000, President Bill Clinton attended a formal signing ceremony of the Arusha Accord. The agreement provided for a three-year *transitional government*. First, a Tutsi would serve as president for an 18-month term, and he would

D

BURUNDI

Pierre Nkurunziza (left), leader of the rebel Forces for Defense of Democracy (FDD), signs a ceasefire agreement with the government of Burundi in late 2003. President Domitien Ndayzeye, like Nkurunziza an ethnic Hutu, is seated at the right.

be followed by a Hutu who would also serve as president for 18 months. Open elections would follow.

Although the civil war in Burundi was officially ended with the signing of the 2000 Arusha Accord, in reality conditions were as bad as ever. The renegade FDD and FROLINA kept on fighting, and the civil war in Burundi was no closer to a resolution than it had been after the coup attempt of 1993.

Mandela pressed on, negotiating with President Buyoya and FRODEBU officials in the summer of 2001. With Mandela's assistance, the transitional government was scheduled to take over on November 1 of that year. Although the Tutsi in UPRONA disagreed as to who should be Burundi's first transitional president, Buyoya won the post because he had the army's support. A transitional National Assembly took office. Politicians who had fled Burundi during the decade of unrest were among those appointed to the new assembly, and they came home under military protection.

The FDD and FROLINA continued their campaign of violence in Burundi. On December 2, 2002, the FDD signed a ceasefire treaty with the government. This has not entirely stopped fighting with the military, or targeting of innocent civilians. Attacks by rebel groups are still a danger, particularly in the areas around Bujumbura. Even religious leaders are not safe. On December 29, 2003, Monsignor Michael Courtney, a representative of the Roman Catholic pope in Burundi, was shot and killed in a car while on the way to Bujumbura. In February 2004, a young rebel soldier admitted FROLINA's involvement after being arrested.

In April 2003, a Hutu named Domitien Ndayizeye took over the presidency from Buyoya. As president, during 2004 he undertook negotiations with members of FROLINA. The peace process was being brokered by the Netherlands. Although both parties expressed a commitment to end the violence in Burundi, FROLINA ignored a deadline set by the government for continuing negotiations.

The Government of Burundi Today

The government of Burundi can be separated into three branches: legislative, executive, and judicial. The legislative branch is responsible for making the laws; the executive branch enforces the laws and proposes new legislation; and the judicial branch interprets the laws.

The president is the head of the executive branch, so the person in that position has a great deal of power. The president is the chief of state and oversees Burundi's government. A prime minister, appointed by the president, helps to run the country. The president chooses ministers to take charge over various departments of the government, such as agriculture, labor, and defense. These ministers are the main advisors for the president and prime minister. The president appoints ambassadors who manage Burundi's relations with other countries. The president controls the military and is responsible for seeing that the judicial system is working fairly. The president can also suggest laws for the National Assembly to approve.

The chief of state in Burundi is president Domitien Ndayizeye; his term as president is scheduled to run until the fall of 2004, when the transitional government ends. His vice president, Alphonse Kadege, was chosen from the Tutsi minority.

The National Assembly is Burundi's lawmaking body. In addition to passing all of the country's laws, the National Assembly must approve all taxes and plans for government spending. To keep the president from having too much power, the National Assembly has the right to investigate corruption in the executive branch of government.

The 1998 transitional constitution expanded the number of seats in the National Assembly from 121 to 140. No elections have been held in Burundi since 1993. The current members of the assembly were appointed in the fall of 2001. After the three-year period of transitional government is completed, members of the National Assembly are to be elected by popular vote to serve five-year terms.

The court system includes 123 small local courts called tribunals of first instance. There are also 17 provincial courts of first instance where more important matters are judged. Decisions in these courts can be overruled or upheld by one of the three national courts of appeal. Burundi has a Constitutional Court, in which matters relating to law and government are debated. Finally, there is a Supreme Court, which is the final word on matters of *jurisprudence*.

The Council of the Bashingantahe for National Unity and Reconciliation is an independent advisory body that can be consulted by the president or ministers as well as members of the National Assembly. The purpose of this organization is to promote greater unity in Burundi and better understanding between the Hutu and Tutsi. The Council of the Bashingantahe proposes ways to maintain a peaceful and just society in Burundi.

UPRONA and FRODEBU remain the two largest political parties in Burundi, but since 1998 a number of new parties have begun participating in government. These include the Burundi African Alliance for the Salvation (ABASA), Rally for Democracy and Economic and Social Development (RADDES), Party for National Redress (PARENA), and the People's Reconciliation Party (PRP).

The Arusha Accord calls for direct elections by the end of November 2004. However, the agreement set certain preconditions before elections could take place. Most important is a legitimate cease-fire in Burundi's seemingly endless civil war. Other conditions include an accurate census of the population and the distribution of forgery-proof identification cards to all voters. It seems likely the country may miss this deadline, as Burundi still has a long way to go to achieve stability and lasting peace.

(Opposite) Agriculture is an important part of Burundi's economy. The two women pictured here are picking cotton. (Right) A Hutu woman waits in line to purchase flour and rice. Poverty is a major problem in Burundi, as approximately seven of every ten people cannot afford food and other necessities.

4 A Struggling Economy

BECAUSE BURUNDI has been devastated by years of unrest, it does not have much of an economy. The country has few natural resources other than its rich soil, and the only ports it has operate on the shore of Lake Tanganyika in Bujumbura. Furthermore, even before the violence that has held Burundi back began, the country's manufacturing base was not well developed.

Although the capital of Bujumbura was modern and efficient before a decade of civil war, the country as a whole lacks the *infrastructure* to develop new businesses. There are no railroads, relatively few paved roads, and only one airport with a paved runway. Electrical service is sporadic, and power lines are mainly located around cities. Communications are also limited. In this country of some six million people there are fewer than 20,000 land-line telephones. Burundi has just five radio stations and

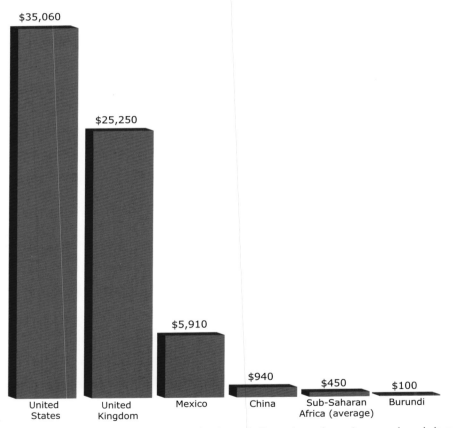

Gross National Income (GNI) Per Capita of Burundi and Other Countries*

$35,060 — United States

$25,250 — United Kingdom

$5,910 — Mexico

$940 — China

$450 — Sub-Saharan Africa (average)

$100 — Burundi

*Gross national income per capita is the total value of all goods and services produced domestically in a year, supplemented by income received from abroad, divided by midyear population. The above figures take into account fluctuations in currency exchange rates and differences in inflation rates across global economies.

Figures are 2002 estimates. Source: World Bank, 2003

one government-run television station that broadcasts to perhaps 30,000 television sets. In 2002, the latest year for which figures are available, only 6,000 people in Burundi had access to the Internet.

Overall, about 70 percent of all Burundians—both Hutu and Tutsi—live in poverty. The average rural Burundian does not get to eat very much meat, for instance, surviving mostly on root vegetables, tubers, and grains like corn and sorghum. The annual per capita income is about $100, although in rural areas many people earn much less. (By comparison, the average person in the U.S. makes about $35,000 a year.)

Burundi's Economy

About 90 percent of all Burundians make their living in whole or in part through *subsistence farming*. Rural families grow their food on plots of land that are usually three acres or smaller. Crops include bananas, cassava, manioc, corn, yams, and sorghum.

About 13 percent of Burundi's land is permanently dedicated to growing crops. A large proportion of the remaining land is used as pastureland for Tutsi cattle. In remote areas, Tutsi families sometimes still allow Hutu families to farm their land in exchange for a share of their crops. The image of the Tutsi elite versus the Hutu peasant, however, is often truest to life in urban areas, where Tutsi generally enjoy better education and social organization. In the country, most Tutsi are just as poor as their Hutu counterparts.

Agriculture contributes about half the value of Burundi's *gross domestic product* (GDP), the total value of goods and services produced in the country each year. In 2002, the most recent year for which accurate figures are available,

Coffee trees grow on a plantation in Burundi. Coffee is one of the country's major export crops.

Burundi's GDP was about $3.146 billion. In addition to the food Burundians grow for their own consumption, the major agricultural products are coffee, tea, sugar, cotton, and cattle hides that can be turned into leather.

Coffee and tea are the country's largest cash crops, and the most important of Burundi's exports. Burundi earns about $26 million from international trade each year, and coffee and tea exports account for approximately 90 percent of this total. Therefore, the country's economy depends on good weather and healthy trees free from parasites, as well as on international prices for coffee and other commodities. A bad year for the coffee crop would be a major blow to Burundi's economy. (It is another sign of the ethnic imbalance in the country that Tutsi dominate the lucrative business of coffee and tea farming.)

Industry contributes about 19 percent to Burundi's GDP, although this figure has grown in recent years. Most of the manufacturing jobs available are for unskilled workers. Factories in Burundi make consumer goods such as soap and blankets, process and package food, and assemble products using imported parts. There is also some construction work through a governmental public-works program.

The service sector of Burundi's economy, which includes retail, hospitality, and tourism jobs, makes up 31 percent of the GDP. However, most Burundians' job prospects are limited because of the lack of educational

Quick Facts: The Economy of Burundi

Gross domestic product (GDP*):
$3.146 billion

Inflation: 12%

Natural Resources: nickel, uranium, rare earth oxides, peat, cobalt, copper, platinum, vanadium; arable land and hydropower

Agriculture (50% of GDP): coffee, cotton, tea, corn, sorghum, sweet potatoes, bananas, manioc, beef, milk, hides

Industry (19% of GDP): light consumer goods such as blankets, shoes, soap; assembly of imported components; public works construction; food processing

Services (31% of GDP): retail, tourism, banking, government

Foreign Trade:

Exports–$26 million: coffee, tea, sugar, cotton, hides

Imports–$135 million: capital goods, petroleum products, foodstuffs

Economic Growth Rate: 4.5%

Currency Exchange Rate: 1,074.64 Burundi francs = U.S. $1 (June 2004)

*GDP, or gross domestic product, is the total value of goods and services produced in a country annually.

All figures are 2002 estimates unless otherwise indicated.

Sources: CIA World Factbook, 2003; Bloomberg.com.

opportunities in the country. Even though in recent years cease-fires have ended some of the ethnic violence, only about half of all Burundian children go to school, and the educated people are disproportionately Tutsi. About half of all Burundians aged 15 and up can read and write, but men are more likely to be literate than women. About 59 percent of men can read and write, compared to 45 percent of women.

The shortage of educated workers and the lack of infrastructure hold back Burundi's economy. Because of Burundi's lack of natural resources, the country also needs to import many goods into the country, including food, manufactured items, and petroleum products. The trade imbalance, coupled with the problems of war and disease that Burundi must cope with, means that the country requires economic and humanitarian aid to feed its people. In addition to more than $92 million a year in foreign aid, Burundi has accumulated an international debt of more than $1.1 billion. It is unlikely that the country will be able to repay any of this debt in the foreseeable future.

The Impact of Disease on the Economy

Clean food and water are not always easy to find in Burundi, resulting in high rates of the parasitic disease *schistosomiasis* and a bacterial infection called *cholera*. Throughout sub-Saharan Africa *malaria* is a widespread problem, although in Burundi cases of this illness tend to be concentrated along the shores of lakes and rivers, leaving the rest of the country relatively free of the disease. Tuberculosis is another widespread problem, as Burundi has one of the highest rates of death from this disease in the world. Burundians are also subject to illnesses resulting from nutritional deficiencies, such as *kwashiorkor*, a childhood condition caused by a diet too low in protein. Symptoms include retarded growth, diarrhea, lightening of the skin and hair, and, in fatal cases, liver failure.

Unfortunately, medical care is not available for many Burundians. Reports show that on average there is one doctor for every 30,000 people in the country. The truth is that because most doctors are concentrated in the cities, most of Burundi's population has no access to health care. As a result, disease and illnesses have taken a great toll on Burundi's potential work force.

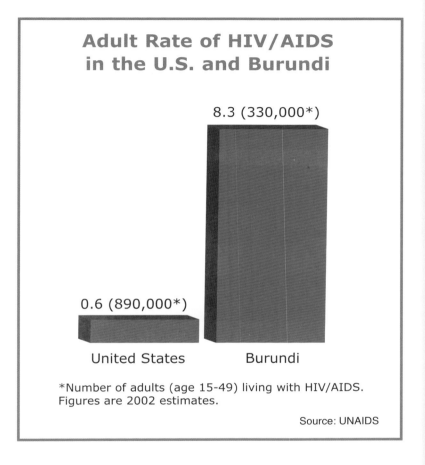

Adult Rate of HIV/AIDS in the U.S. and Burundi

8.3 (330,000*)

0.6 (890,000*)

United States   Burundi

*Number of adults (age 15-49) living with HIV/AIDS. Figures are 2002 estimates.

Source: UNAIDS

The disease that has most devastated the economy is AIDS, the modern-day scourge of sub-Saharan Africa. Burundi's first AIDS case was diagnosed in 1983; since then, infection rates have soared. Today, it is estimated that more than 8 percent of Burundi's adult population is infected with HIV, the

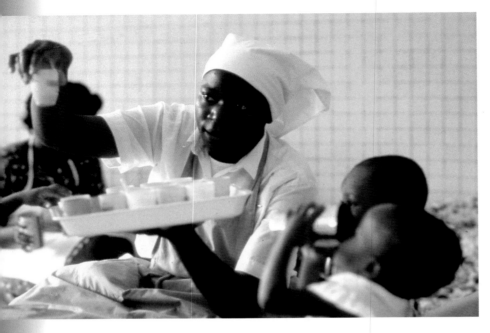

A nun cares for children affected with AIDS. Diseases like tuberculosis, malaria, and AIDS have a great impact on the economy of Burundi because they take young adult workers out of the labor force.

virus that causes AIDS. This is among the highest infection rates in the world. There are approximately 40,000 AIDS-related deaths in the tiny republic each year, prompting Dr. Joseph Wakana, executive secretary to Burundi's National AIDS Council, to announce in June 2001, "AIDS has become the leading cause of mortality among children and adults in this country."

Infection rates tend to be highest in Burundi's cities, where 13 percent of all women and 5.5 percent of all men are HIV positive. The infection rate is climbing quickly in rural areas, particularly among young girls and women. Displaced refugees living in camps within Burundi also have high rates of HIV infection. Since the 1980s, approximately 240,000 children under age 15 have lost parents to the disease.

If the spread of AIDS continues unchecked in Burundi, it will further devastate the already-weak economy by removing hundreds of thousands of adults from the labor force during their prime working years. The disease shortens the lives of infected workers. The United Nations projects that Burundi's average life expectancy will be less than 40 years by 2010 unless infection rates drop.

The best treatment for prolonging the lives of people with HIV or AIDS is a class of drugs called antiretrovirals (ARVs). The cheapest price for an ARV regimen in Burundi is about $360 per year—far too high for most Burundians to afford. For a lucky few, financial assistance is available. At the end of 2003, Health Minister Dr. Jean Kumana approved health insurance coverage for HIV-positive civil servants that will pay 80 percent of their treatment costs. Unfortunately, there is not enough money or medicine for the hundreds of thousands of Burundians who have already been infected with HIV. Burundi's government will have to do more to stop the spread of AIDS and care for its people who have the disease if it hopes to keep the country's economy from collapsing in the future.

The violence in Burundi has taken a terrible toll on society. (Opposite) The Bwiza neighborhood of Bujumbura was once home to both Hutu and Tutsi families, but by 1995 the Tutsi had killed or driven out all of the Hutu residents. (Right) Despite the tragedy of the civil war, there are happy moments in the country, such as this Tutsi wedding.

5 A Culture of Mistrust

HOSPITALITY WAS ONCE an important part of Burundian culture, although the decades of ethnic violence have turned hospitality to mistrust. Despite the country's problems, the people of Burundi still have a rich legacy of family traditions and fine arts.

The landscape of Burundi contributes to close family ties because it is so hilly. Historically, small, tightly knit groups of people lived in communities on different hills, separated by lower valleys. Men and women have different responsibilities in Burundian society. The husband is the head of the household, and in rural areas is responsible for building and maintaining the family home. This is usually a small hut made of wood with a tin roof, although some houses are made of concrete blocks. The houses are in an enclosed space called a *rugo*, where cows and other livestock are kept. Men are also responsible for tending cattle or livestock, while women are responsible for cultivating crops as well as raising children.

Parents are very involved in their children's choice of a spouse. In rural areas, the "bride price"—the gift that the groom's family presents to the bride's family—may still take the form of hides, cattle, or farming equipment. In urban areas, these gifts may be money, clothes, or household supplies. The two families meet and seal the engagement with beer, which is drunk at almost all social events. It may be malt beer, which is brewed commercially, or a home-brewed sorghum beer called *impeke*.

When a Burundian couple has a baby, they generally do not name the child right away. This is a tradition that developed in part because of Burundi's high infant mortality rate. As a result of the lack of health care in much of the country, 7 percent of all newborns die within the first year. This is more than 10 times higher than the rate in the United States and other developed countries. Because of disease, malnutrition, and war most Burundians do not live long lives. The average life expectancy in the country is about 43 years, which is 30 to 40 years shorter than the life expectancy of people living in industrialized nations.

European missionaries brought Christianity to the Burundi region during the 19th century, and today two-thirds of Burundians are Christian. Most of these are Roman Catholics, but there is a growing population of Protestant or Evangelical Christians. Burundi also has a community of people who follow Islam; Muslims are estimated at about 10 percent of the population. The remaining 23 percent of the people follow tribal religions, most of which are rooted in *animist* beliefs. In many cases Christian and Muslim rituals have influenced the practice of tribal religions.

Quick Facts: The People of Burundi

Population: 6,096,156
Ethnic Groups: Hutu, 85%; Tutsi, 14%; Twa, 1%; small communities of Europeans and South Asians
Age structure:
  0–14 years: 46.7%
  15–64 years: 50.6%
  65 years and over: 2.7%
Population growth rate: 2.18%
Birth rate: 39.72 births/1,000 population
Infant mortality rate: 71.54 deaths/1,000 live births
Death rate: 17.8 deaths/1,000 population
Total fertility rate: 5.99 children born/woman

Life expectancy at birth:
  total population: 43.2 years
  male: 42.54 years
  female: 43.88 years
Religion: Christian 67% (Roman Catholic 62%, Protestant 5%); indigenous beliefs, 23%; Muslim 10%
Languages: Kirundi (official), French (official), Swahili
Literacy (percentage of people age 15 and over who can read and write): 51.6%

All figures are 2003 estimates unless otherwise indicated.
Source: Adapted from CIA World Factbook, 2003.

During the 1920s, the Belgians forced Burundians to carry identification cards that registered them as Hutu or Tutsi. Because of intermarriage and social status, the Belgian registration program was not completely accurate. In 1956, a demographic survey of Burundians attempted to sort the Hutu from the Tutsi. Once again, though, this study was not very scientific: a family might be counted as Tutsi if its members were tall or owned a few cows, regardless of their ethnic history. The study failed to take into account that many Tutsi were small-scale farmers and some Hutu owned cattle. Today, the Hutu population is estimated at about

85 percent, with the Tutsi at 14 percent and the Twa a small minority of about 1 percent.

Until European colonization, there was no written form of Kirundi, Burundi's official language. Many Burundians also speak the republic's second official language, French, and can understand Kinyarwanda, the language of the Rwandan Hutu and Tutsi, which is almost identical to Kirundi. In addition, many can at least understand Swahili, the language of commerce along Lake Tanganyika's shores.

A group of nuns walk in front of the church at Mushasha. About 67 percent of the people living in Burundi follow Christianity. Most are Roman Catholics, but there are a growing number of Protestant Christians.

Education and Cultural Opportunities

The Christian missionaries who built schools and churches in Burundi during the late 19th and early 20th centuries were aware of the tension between Hutu and Tutsi. Most of the students who were educated in mission schools were Tutsi, because the colonial administrators favored them. Today, Burundi's primary schools are supposed to be free to all children between seven and twelve years old. However, just under half of all children in Burundi attend primary schools, and a higher percentage of these students are Tutsi. Of the Hutu children who attend primary school, few earn admission to secondary school.

Equal access to secondary education for Hutu children is an emotionally charged issue. Some international charitable organizations subsidize vocational and trade schools for youth in Bujumbura, Gitega, and other towns for young people who are unable to attend secondary school. At these schools, the mostly Hutu student body gets a chance to learn a trade, such as carpentry.

The few students who complete secondary schools can continue their studies at the University of Burundi, which was founded in 1960. The school, located in Bujumbura, employs some 400 professors and has a student enrollment of more than 3,000. In addition to offering traditional college degrees, the University of Burundi also has a medical school and professional training programs for teachers and engineers. Bujumbura also has schools for foreign students, most of whom are the children of embassy personnel.

An unfortunate side effect of the civil war in Burundi was that many children were sucked into the fighting. Hutu rebels would kidnap children as young as age 10 and force them to carry ammunition and supplies, fight in battles, and work as spies. The national army also *conscripted* young people during the conflict. Although no one knows exactly how many children were drawn into the conflict, the United Nations Children's Fund (UNICEF) estimated in 2004 that between 6,000 and 7,000 child soldiers remained mobilized. Because these children were not educated, it will be difficult for them to contribute to Burundian society in a positive way. "Regardless of how they were recruited, child soldiers are likely to have witnessed or participated in extreme violence, as well as to have been the object of abuse," said a March 2004 report by the international human-rights organization Amnesty International. "The legacy of children having spent years

These students at a Bujumbura school are participating in a peace education class. The purpose of the program is to promote greater understanding between the Hutu and Tutsi.

within the armed forces, primarily learning the art of violence, will have lasting repercussions on the country and its citizens unless the problem is urgently addressed."

Cultural Pursuits in Burundi

Most of Burundi's schools and museums are concentrated in the country's two main cities. The capital is home to the Bujumbura Living Museum, along with the American Cultural Center and the French Cultural Center. Gitega is home to an art school and a research library called the Burundi Literature Center. The National Museum is also located in Gitega. Given Burundi's desperate economic situation, however, little money is available to fund cultural activities or facilities.

Music is one form of entertainment that all Burundians enjoy. The Hutu have a song for almost every occasion: the birth of a child, harvesting crops, rebuking community members who are misbehaving, or even for paddling a canoe against strong currents. The songs fall into social, ceremonial, and religious categories. The Tutsi sing songs that reflect the important things in their lives. They sing specific songs as they feed and water their cattle and as they lead them back into the *rugo* at night.

Burundi is home to one type of singing not found anywhere else in the world, *inanga chuchotee*, or "whispered singing." A singer whispers a song while accompanied by a stringed instrument called the *inanga* (also known as a tree zither), which is made from the wood of the *ikivumu* tree. Whispered singing is much harder than it sounds. The singer must make it seem as if his or her voice has variations in pitch—something that is impossible to do while

Drummers leap high in the air while performing a folk dance. Music and dancing are very important to Burundian society.

whispering. To be successful, the singer's voice must blend seamlessly with the tonal changes in the music played on the *inanga*, so that it sounds as if the whispering varies in tone and pitch like regular singing.

The instruments Burundians have traditionally chosen to accompany their songs are largely percussive. The Karyenda drum may be the oldest instrument. Made of wood with a cowhide stretched over the top, this drum once figured prominently in folk songs and dances that praised the monarchy.

Karyenda drums were once sacred: it was a privilege to be able to play one and release the drum's unique spirit and voice. Other Burundian instruments include the *umuduri*, a single-stringed instrument shaped like a bow; the *inyagara*, or rattle; and a finger piano called the *ikembe*.

Dance naturally follows instrumental music. Like singing, dance serves ceremonial purposes, as well as the purpose of having fun. One dance called the *abatimbo* commonly accompanies both informal and ceremonial celebrations. *Intore* dancers perform in striking costume, doing the dances that once entertained Burundi's kings. The Drummers of Burundi, a touring 14-person group that is famous around the world, incorporates both drumming and dancing into their shows. Many more Burundians drum and dance just as Americans play competitive sports.

Unlike Burundi's musical forms of expression, basket-weaving and pottery are crafts that have traditionally been done by women. Beautifully made baskets are a source of pride in Burundian households. But they are not mere showpieces; they are made to do everything from holding food at the table to heavier work outdoors. Women weave and coil their baskets out of papyrus fibers, using dyes made from mud or plants to incorporate geometrical designs in them—making dark purplish designs against a tan background, for example.

Many of Burundi's most skilled potters are Twa women. They use earthen clay, fired to a glossy black finish, to make their pots. Like baskets, the pots are meant to be used, rather than displayed. Burundian women use their pottery to store food and grain and to hold drinks.

(Opposite) A rainbow lights the sky over Bujumbura. Burundi's largest city is home to about 340,000 people. (Right) Most of the people of Burundi live in rural villages.

6 Cities and Communities

Although Burundi is densely populated, less than 10 percent of the country's 6 million inhabitants live in cities. There are only two communities in Burundi that can legitimately be called cities. One is Bujumbura, the national capital, with a 2004 population of approximately 340,000 people. The other is Gitega, with a population of just 47,000.

Burundi is divided into 16 provinces: Bubanza, Bujumbura, Bururi, Cankuzo, Cibitoke, Gitega, Karuzi, Kayanza, Kirundo, Makamba, Muramvya, Muyinga, Mwaro, Ngozi, and Rutana. Each province has a governor, who is appointed by the president; the provinces are further divided into districts that each include more than 100 villages or towns. At the local level, the district and local authorities are often Tutsi.

Bujumbura

Known as Usumbura until Burundi's independence, this city on the northern shore of Lake Tanganyika was established as a German military station in 1899. When Belgium took over the administration of Ruanda-Urundi, Usumbura became the colony's center of operations. Today, Bujumbura is home to the National Assembly as well as Burundi's high court, the Tribunal de Grande Instance. Produce, livestock, and handcrafts from farmers and artisans outside the city are for sale in Bujumbura's open-air markets. Most of the country's manufacturing takes place in the capital, and the city's international airport and port on Lake Tanganyika make it Burundi's center of commerce.

Unfortunately, there are two parts of Bujumbura. One is a relatively luxurious city of beachfront hotels and fancy restaurants frequented by the Tutsi elite and foreign businesspeople and diplomats. The other was once home to working-class Tutsi and Hutu, but it now is a ruined city ruled by unpredictable violence.

Fighting in the city—especially after the 1993 assassination of Ndadaye—has periodically disrupted manufacturing, education, and other aspects of life in an urban center. Before the civil war began, many younger Burundians living, working, and studying in Bujumbura did classify themselves by their ethnicity. Today, however, there are practically no Hutu living in Bujumbura. During the war the army, as well as violent gangs of Tutsi, systematically "purified" the city neighborhood by neighborhood. Hutu may straggle in from the hills above the capital to work or shop, but they make it a point to leave before dark.

The Tutsi-dominated military in Burundi has set up posts throughout the country to make sure people are not carrying weapons. The soldiers are supposed to protect Hutu residents traveling through Tutsi districts from being robbed, beaten, or killed. However, because most of the soldiers are Tutsi, the system sometimes breaks down.

For Tutsi, the price of staying in the city has been high: many were forced to leave their homes and take shelter under the protection of the army in displaced person camps or in churches, schools, and other buildings large enough to house a lot of people. Just as the Hutu fear the Tutsi-dominated army, the Tutsi live in fear of Hutu rebel groups, who have killed civilians and even abducted children from schools for use as child soldiers.

Gitega

Gitega is about 40 miles (65 km) east of Bujumbura, and is connected to the capital by a highway. The second-largest city in Burundi is also the capital of Gitega Province. Although Gitega is much smaller than Bujumbura, it has a storied past and great cultural significance. Gitega was once home to the *mwamis* who ruled Burundi, and today visitors to Gitega's National Museum can see many artifacts from the Burundian royal court. Gitega is home to the archbishop of Gitega, the head of the Roman Catholic Church in Burundi. The city also has active Protestant and Muslim communities.

Under Belgian rule, Gitega became the first city where coffee was cultivated. One of the country's largest coffee processing factories is located in Gitega. The city's other industries include trading in livestock, tanning leather, and peat mining. Peat is made from decomposed plant material; it can be processed into briquettes of fuel, like coal.

One of the worst massacres in the vicinity of Gitega occurred on September 9, 2002. The Burundian army, which was chasing Hutu rebels, told civilians living in the hills of Kangoma and Kanyonga to evacuate their homes. The civilians did not trust the government; fearing they would be sent to *regroupment* camps, they did not leave. When the military launched an attack against the rebels, 173 civilians were killed in the crossfire.

New Ways to Build Integrated Communities

The city of Ngozi, which is located near crowded and unsanitary refugee camps, may not be very large, but it may one day serve as a model to bring

Hutu and Tutsi together for the common good. Catholic, Protestant, and Muslim religious leaders and villagers in the province of Ngozi raised $600,000 to start a community bank. Hutu and Tutsi of all classes paid roughly $10 apiece to become stakeholders. Their venture, called the Company for Finance and Development, cut across ethnic lines by financing the rebuilding of the war-torn province.

Ngozi resident and former prime minister Anatole Kanyenkiko was one of the company's founders. "If you and I are shareholders in a business, together we will protect our business and each other instead of destroying it and killing ourselves," he explained. To receive funding, residents of the Ngozi province must form integrated committees and propose projects that will benefit both the Hutu and Tutsi communities.

One of the Company for Finance and Development's greatest cooperative endeavors has been the creation of the University of Ngozi in 1999, tapping part-time professors from Bujumbura University to teach. A coffee factory also now operates in Ngozi thanks to the community bank. Tutsi and Hutu have worked together to finance the rebuilding of schools, hospitals, and neighborhoods destroyed by fighting. As a result of their efforts, incidents of violence have decreased dramatically in the area.

The triumph of Ngozi in the face of ethnic fighting is a small one, but it represents the marriage of economic development and interethnic peace that Burundi desperately needs if it is to have a sustainable future.

A Calendar of Burundian Festivals

January

On January 1, Burundians celebrate **New Year's Day**. During this holiday, families and friends get together for dinner, or to enjoy music and dancing.

February

Burundi celebrates **Unity Day** on February 5. This holiday commemorates February 5, 1991, which was the first day of a transition to democracy that led to election of Melchior Ndadaye.

The date of **Ash Wednesday** varies from year to year, and sometimes falls in March rather than February. This festival marks the beginning of the season of **Lent**, which last for 40 days. During Lent Roman Catholics are expected to spend extra time praying and reflecting on spiritual matters.

March/April

The last week of Lent is known as Passion Week, and commemorates the arrival of Jesus in Jerusalem on **Palm Sunday**, the Last Supper on **Holy Thursday**, and the crucifixion on **Good Friday**. These are followed by **Easter Sunday**, when Christians celebrate the resurrection of Jesus. The dates of these holidays vary from year to year; Easter always falls between March 22 and April 25. The Monday after Easter is also a public holiday.

May

On May 1, Burundians celebrate **Labor Day**, a holiday for working-class people.

June

Christians celebrate **Ascension Day**, which commemorates the day Jesus ascended into heaven. This holiday is held 40 days after Easter Sunday, so its date varies from year to year, and it is sometimes held in May.

July

On July 1, Burundians celebrate **Independence Day,** which marks the anniversary of Burundi's independence from Belgium in 1962. Government leaders give speeches throughout the country, and many official functions are scheduled to mark this day.

August

A popular Christian feast is the **Assumption of the Virgin Mary** on August 15. Roman Catholics observe this festival in honor of Mary, the mother of Jesus, whose body is believed to have been taken into heaven after her death.

September

Victory of UPRONA Day on September 18 marks the anniversary of the 1961 victory of UPRONA in Burundi's first elections.

October

On October 13, Burundians observe **Prince Rwagasore Day** (also called Murder of the Hero Day). This is a remembrance of the 1961 assassination of Louis Rwagasore.

President Ndadaye Day, held October 21, is

A Calendar of Burundian Festivals

a remembrance of the 1993 assassination of Melchior Ndadaye. Both of these national holidays are commemorated by ceremonies in which wreaths are laid on the tombs of the two leaders.

November

On November 1, Christians in Burundi observe **All Saint's Day**.

The **Anniversary of the Revolution**, which commemorates Burundi's 1966 declaration as a republic, is celebrated on November 30.

December

Burundian Christians observe **Christmas** on December 25.

During the last week of December, people clean and decorate their homes in preparation for the new year.

Other Festivals and Holidays

Because Islam follows a lunar calendar that is 10 or 11 days shorter than the solar year, Muslims observe their religious holy days at different times of the year. The most significant month of the Muslim lunar calendar is the ninth month, **Ramadan**. This is a time of sacrifice for devout Muslims. During Ramadan, Muslims are not supposed to eat or drink between sunup and sundown. They are also supposed to restrict their activities during these hours to necessary duties, such as going to work. After the sun has set completely, Muslims recite a special prayer before eating a small meal.

Ramadan ends with a three-day festival called **Eid al-Fitr**, or Feast of Fast-Breaking. During this time families get together and exchange gifts.

The **Eid al-Adha**, or Feast of Sacrifice, is a more serious occasion. It takes place at the end of the *hajj* period, during which Muslims make their way to Mecca on pilgrimage. Eid al-Adha commemorates the willingness of the patriarch Abraham to sacrifice his son to God. In the story, God provided a sheep for the sacrifice, and according to tradition Muslim families should slaughter and eat a sheep on this day.

Burundians also observe a traditional fertility and harvest festival called **Umugamuro**, which is held in the fall.

Recipes

Biltong (dried meat)

beef sliced into thin strips
rock salt
2 cups vinegar
black pepper
coriander

Directions:

1. Sprinkle the rock salt onto the beef strips and let them stand for at least an hour.
2. Scrape the extra salt off the strips, then dip them completely into the vinegar. Lay the strips onto a towel or wire rack.
3. After the excess vinegar has dripped off the beef strips, sprinkle them with pepper and coriander.
4. Let beef dry for several days until hard.

Beef and Cassava Leaves

Three cups of washed cassava leaves
red pepper
1 pound of stew meat
3/4 cup of peanut butter
peanut oil

Directions:

1. Boil cassava leaves.
2. Sauté stew meat with peanut oil in a separate pot. When the meat is browned, reduce heat and add the cassava to the pot with the meat and oil.
3. Let the mixture simmer until the cassava is tender.
4. Drain the mixture, then return it to the pot.
5. Add peanut butter and heat again until warm.

Spinach Potatoes

4 peeled potatoes
2 cups chopped spinach leaves
1 cup olive oil
1 teaspoon garlic powder
2 cups of chickpeas
2 diced green peppers
1 diced red onion
1 teaspoon oregano
1 teaspoon basil

Directions:

1. Boil potatoes until tender.
2. Add spinach and cook a few more minutes.
3. Drain water.
4. Using a deep pan, heat olive oil to a gentle boil.
5. Add potato and spinach mixture, as well as the remaining ingredients.
6. Sauté for five minutes. Reduce heat, cover, and simmer for a few more minutes.

Bananas and Beans

16-ounce can of kidney beans
4 peeled bananas
2 tablespoons palm oil
1 finely chopped onion
dash of salt
3 cups water

Directions:
1. Peel and slice bananas.
2. Brown onion in palm oil.
3. Add the bananas, beans, and salt to onion and oil and sauté for three minutes.
4. Pour in three cups of water and simmer mixture until bananas are cooked and most of the water has evaporated. Serve right away.

Fried Beans

1 pound white haricot beans, washed
1/2 cup peanut oil
3 sliced onions
1 crushed garlic clove
1 heaping teaspoon salt
1 dried chili pepper

Directions:
1. Boil beans in deep saucepan for three minutes.
2. Turn off heat and soak beans in pot of water for two hours.
3. Turn heat back on to low and simmer beans till tender.
4. In a frying pan, sauté onions and garlic in peanut oil until onions are clear.
5. Drain beans and add to frying pan.
6. Cook for five more minutes.
7. Remove from heat and mix in salt and chili pepper.

Glossary

animism—a belief that all things in nature, such as trees and animals, possess spirits and consciousness.

biodiversity—variety of plant and animal life.

cassava—type of plant having starchy roots that can be used to make flour; the leaves are also edible.

cholera—a potentially lethal bacterial illness caused by ingesting contaminated food and water.

client-patron relationship—a relationship in which one group of people is entirely dependent on, and therefore ruled by, another group.

conscript—to forcibly enroll someone in the military.

eleusine—a type of cereal grain.

endemic—only found in a particular region.

gross domestic product—the total value of all goods and services produced in a country during a specific period of time, such as a year.

indirect rule—the practice of taking over and ruling a colony by choosing a native chief, leader or king, to enforce the policies of the conquering nation.

infrastructure—large-scale public systems, such as power and water supplies, telecommunications, highways and railroads, and schools, that are necessary for economic activity in a country.

inkuka—tribute given to the kings of Burundi before the arrival of Europeans in the 19th century.

jurisprudence—the system of law in a country.

Glossary

landlocked—to be enclosed or nearly enclosed by land, with no access to an ocean.

malaria—a parasitic disease caused by the bite of an infected mosquito that results in prolonged fever.

nullify—to make something of no value or consequence.

patrilineal—tracing descent through the fathers' family.

prime minister—the chief executive of a parliamentary government.

sanctions—a measure taken by one or more nations to apply pressure on another nation to conform to international law or opinion.

savanna—a grassy, tropical plain with few trees or none at all.

schistosomiasis—a parasitic disease in which a type of worm infests the host's body.

sphere of influence—a territorial area within which the political influence of one nation is considered superior to all others.

subsistence farming—farming that generates just enough to feed the farmer's family, with little or nothing left over to sell.

transitional government—a government that is put in place to help lead the country from one stage to another, until a permanent government can be chosen.

Project and Report Ideas

In-Depth Biographical Report

Burundi's most famous citizen is probably track star Venuste Niyongabo. He started as a middle-distance runner—his event was the 1,500 meters—during the early 1990s. But it was as a long-distance runner that he found international fame. In 1996, Niyongabo was one of seven Burundian athletes that comprised that country's very first Olympic team. He, like the rest of his teammates in Atlanta, was a Tutsi. He won a gold medal for Burundi in the 5,000 meters—his country's first Olympic medal. Write a report about Niyongabo's career and achievements, with special focus on the 1996 Olympics. Or, write about Burundi's efforts to field its first Olympic team, and the republic's participation in the Olympics since 1996.

Comparative Report

When an airplane carrying Burundian President Cyprien Ntaryamira and Rwandan President Juvenal Habyarimana was apparently shot down over the Rwandan capital of Kigali on April 6, 1994, the two countries responded to the tragedy very differently. Both presidents were Hutu, and both Burundi and Rwanda have similar ethnic makeups. Write a report that explains how each country's people responded to the suspicious deaths of their respective presidents. Make the comparison in the context of each country's history since Belgian colonial rule.

Exploded Map

Using a photocopier, enlarge the map of Burundi at the beginning of this book, then cut apart the country's 16 provinces. Glue the pieces onto a piece of posterboard. Beside each, write a one-paragraph description of the province, mentioning important cities or locations.

Resource Map

Make a map showing where Burundi's resources are located. This information can be found through research on the internet or an encyclopedia.

Project and Report Ideas

Cooperative Project

In teams, assemble a list of the best web sites for finding out information about Burundi. Devise a rating system. Include a one- or two-sentence summary about the site. Combine these reports in a comprehensive guide to Burundi on the Internet for other classes to use.

History Reports

Write one-page reports explaining these events from Burundi's history:

• The client-patron relationship between Hutu and Tutsi
• The effect of the Treaty of Kiganda
• Belgian introduction of coffee and other crops
• The independence movement of the 1950s
• The assassination of Melchior Ndadaye
• The signing of the Arusha Accord

Biographies

Write a one-page report about one of the following figures from Burundi's history:

• John Hanning Speke
• Mwami Mwezi Gisabo
• Louis Rwagasore
• Mwami Mwambutsa IV
• Michel Micombero
• Jean-Baptist Bagaza

• Pierre Boyoya
• Melchior Ndadaye
• Sylvie Kinigi
• Cyprien Ntaryamira
• Sylvestre Ntibantunganya
• Domitien Ndayizeye

Chronology

1300s	The Tutsi, a cattle-herding people, begin to migrate into Burundi.
ca. 1650	The first Tutsi *mwami*, Ntare Rushatsi I, becomes ruler of Burundi.
1858	Richard Burton and John Hanning Speke explore Lake Tanganyika.
1871	Two German priests set up a mission in present-day Bujumbura.
1894	German Count Gustav Adolf von Gotzen claims Rwanda and surrounding areas for Germany. Burundi and Rwanda are administered jointly by Germany as Ruanda-Urundi.
1916	Belgian troops take control of Ruanda-Urundi from Germany during World War I.
1946	The United Nations decrees that Belgium must prepare Burundi for independence.
1958	Prince Louis Rwagasore founds the Party of National Unity and Progress (UPRONA) with the assistance of Burundian regional chiefs and clergy.
1961	Rwagasore is elected Burundi's first prime minister, but is assassinated before he takes office.
1962	Burundi becomes independent from Belgium on July 1.
1965	UPRONA takes a majority of National Assembly seats. King Mwambutsa appoints a Tutsi prime minister, which outrages the Hutu majority. Hutu retaliate by killing Tutsi in the countryside, until the Tutsi-dominated Burundian army represses the uprising, massacring Hutu in retaliation.
1966	Mwambutsa flees the country; his son Ntare V takes crown. Ntare V's right-hand man, Major Michel Micombero, overthrows him and eventually declares himself president and Burundi a republic.

1972   Hutu attempt a coup against Micombero in April, killing thousands of Tutsi; the army represses the rebellion, killing an estimated 150,000 Hutu.

1976   Colonel Jean-Baptiste Bagaza ousts Micombero and becomes president.

1987   Major Pierre Buyoya takes presidency in military coup.

1993   Melchior Ndadaye, a Hutu of the FRODEBU party, becomes the first democratically elected president in Burundi. He is assassinated by military officers in a coup attempt on October 21, touching off a long civil war in Burundi.

1994   Ndadaye's successor, a Hutu named Cyprien Ntaryamira, is killed along with Rwandan President Juvenal Habyarimana in a plane crash on April 6.

1996   Former Tanzanian President Julius Nyerere convenes first Arusha peace talks between Burundian government and Hutu rebel groups. With the support of the army, Major Pierre Buyoya takes power.

1998   Buyoya sworn in as president of Burundi. Nyerere hosts more talks in Arusha.

2000   The Arusha Accord, which calls for a transitional government, is signed by all parties but the Hutu rebel groups FDD and FROLINA on August 28.

2001   Buyoya sworn in as first transitional president.

2002   FDD signs cease-fire agreement with Burundian government.

2003   Domitien Ndayizeye becomes transitional president in April.

2004   Burundi is behind a schedule set in the Arusha Accord to hold open elections.

2005   The Burundian human-rights group AC-Genocide Cirimoso condemns the U.N. for not acting to stop genocide in Burundi during the 1990s.

2006   Heavy rains, leading to floods and landslides, displace thousands in April and May, but have potential to help crops in some provinces.

Further Reading/Internet Resources

Chrétien, Jean-Pierre. *The Great Lakes of Africa: Two Thousand Years of History.* Translated by Scott Straus. New York: Zone Books, 2003.

Jennings, Christian. *Across the Red River: Rwanda, Burundi and the Heart of Darkness.* London: Phoenix, 2001.

Ould-Abdallah, Ahmedou. *Burundi on the Brink, 1993–95: A UN Special Envoy Reflects on Preventive Diplomacy.* Washington, D.C.: United States Institute of Peace, 2000.

Reyntjens, Filip. *Talking or Fighting? Political Evolution in Rwanda and Burundi.* Uppsala, Sweden: Nordisk Afrikainstituet, 1999.

Wolbers, Marian F. *Burundi.* New York: Chelsea House Publishers, 1989.

History and Geography

http://www2.rnw.nl/rnw/en/features/humanrights/historyburundi.html
www.abacci.com/atlas

Culture and Festivals

www.intercultures.ca/cil-cai/country_insights-en.asp?lvl=8
www.countryquest.com/africa/burundi/culture.htm

Economy and Politics

www.nationbynation.com/Burundi/Links.html
www.cia.gov/cia/publications/factbook/geos/by.html

Travel Information

www.1uptravel.com/international/africa/burundi
www.burundiembassy-usa.org/tourism.html

Embassy of the Republic of Burundi
2233 Wisconsin Avenue NW, Suite 212
Washington, DC 20007
Phone: (202) 342-2574
Fax: (202) 342-2578

U.S. Department of State
Bureau of Consular Affairs
Washington, DC 20520
Phone: 202-647-4000
Website: http://travel.state.gov/travel/tips/brochures/brochures_1218.html

National Democratic Institute for International Affairs
2030 M Street NW, Fifth Floor
Washington, DC 20036-3306
Phone: (202) 728-5500
Fax: (202) 728-5520
Website: http://www.ndi.org/worldwide/cewa/burundi/burundi.asp

Index

Numbers in *bold italic* refer to captions.

Contributors/Picture Credits

Professor Robert I. Rotberg is Director of the Program on Intrastate Conflict and Conflict Resolution at the Kennedy School, Harvard University, and President of the World Peace Foundation. He is the author of a number of books and articles on Africa, including *A Political History of Tropical Africa* and *Ending Autocracy, Enabling Democracy: The Tribulations of Southern Africa.*

Kristine Brennan is a writer and editor who lives in the Philadelphia area with her family. She has written several books for young readers.